2018 SQA Past Papers with Answers

National 5
GERMAN

FREE audio files to accompany this title can be accessed at **www.hoddereducation.co.uk/sqaaudiofiles** You will find the files listed by language and level.

2016, 2017 & 2018 Exams

HODDER GIBSON
AN HACHETTE UK COMPANY

This book contains the official SQA 2016, 2017 and 2018 Exams for National 5 German, with associated SQA-approved answers modified from the official marking instructions that accompany the paper.

In addition the book contains study skills advice. This advice has been specially commissioned by Hodder Gibson, and has been written by experienced senior teachers and examiners in line with the new National 5 syllabus and assessment outlines. This is not SQA material but has been devised to provide further guidance for National 5 examinations.

Hodder Gibson is grateful to the copyright holders, as credited on the final page of the Answer section, for permission to use their material. Every effort has been made to trace the copyright holders and to obtain their permission for the use of copyright material. Hodder Gibson will be happy to receive information allowing us to rectify any error or omission in future editions.

Hachette UK's policy is to use papers that are natural, renewable and recyclable products and made from wood grown in sustainable forests. The logging and manufacturing processes are expected to conform to the environmental regulations of the country of origin.

Orders: please contact Bookpoint Ltd, 130 Park Drive, Milton Park, Abingdon, Oxon OX14 4SE. Telephone: (44) 01235 827827. Fax: (44) 01235 400454. Lines are open 9.00–5.00, Monday to Saturday, with a 24-hour message answering service. Visit our website at www.hoddereducation.co.uk. Hodder Gibson can also be contacted directly at hoddergibson@hodder.co.uk

This collection first published in 2018 by
Hodder Gibson, an imprint of Hodder Education,
An Hachette UK Company
211 St Vincent Street
Glasgow G2 5QY

Typeset by Aptara, Inc.

Printed in the UK

A catalogue record for this title is available from the British Library

ISBN: 978-1-5104-5672-3

2 1

2019 2018

Introduction

National 5 German

You have chosen to add a national qualification in German to your education. Congratulations – it is one of the most sought-after foreign languages for business and trade in Scotland and in Europe.

The course specifications for National 5 German changed in 2017 and Units and Unit Assessments were removed. The only change to the exam papers, however, was the removal of "overall purpose" questions for Reading and Listening. The 2017 and 2018 Past Papers reflect this, and the 2016 paper remains an incredibly useful revision tool.

The questions contained in this book of Past Papers provide excellent representative exam practice. Using them as part of your revision will help you to learn the vital skills and techniques needed for the exam and will help you identify any knowledge gaps you may have, prior to the exam season in May–June.

It is always a very good idea to refer to SQA's website for the most up-to-date course specification documents. These are available at www.sqa.org.uk/sqa/47415

What can National 5 do for you?

National 5 German is a course which has been developed by teachers and educational leaders to meet the requirements for Modern Foreign Languages in the 21st century.

The aim of the course is to give you confidence in understanding (reading and listening) and using (talking and writing) German in the following contexts:

- Society (Family and friends, Lifestyle, Media, Global languages, Citizenship)
- Learning (Learning in context, Education)
- Employability (Jobs, Work and CVs)
- Culture (Planning a trip, Other countries, Celebrating a special event, German literature, German films and TV)

What does the Course Assessment look like?

Reading and Writing

You will have 1 hour and 30 minutes for both parts of this paper. This question paper will have 50 marks in total – 37.5% of the overall course marks.

The Reading paper

The reading part of this paper will have 30 marks – 10 marks for each text.

You will read three German texts of between 150 and 200 words each. Questions on the text are set in English, and you must respond in English. These questions will ask for specific details about the text.

You may use a dictionary in this paper.

The Writing paper

You will produce one written text, a job application in German, in response to a stimulus supported by six bullet points which you must address. See them as a checklist of information that you will have to provide in your response.

Four of the bullet points are predictable but two of them are less predictable as they vary from year to year.

The text you produce must take the form of an e-mail and should be between 120 and 150 words in length.

You may use a dictionary in this paper.

You will also have to produce an essay in class which will be sent away to be marked by the SQA.

You can write about anything you want or your teacher may provide you with a topic to write about.

You should write 120–200 words in German and it must be your own work.

You can use your jotters, a dictionary or a word list to help you, but you are not allowed to use textbooks or vocabulary sheets with sentences on it.

Your teacher is allowed to correct your work using a correction code, which you can use to help you redraft.

Your final draft will make up half of your writing mark.

Listening

The Listening paper

This question paper will have 20 marks – 25% of the total mark.

You will listen to one monologue (approximately one and a half minutes long) and one short dialogue (approximately two to two and a half minutes long) in German. You will be asked questions in English and must respond in English.

The monologue is worth 8 marks and the dialogue is worth 12 marks. The dialogue will be linked to the context to the monologue.

You may not use a dictionary in this paper.

Talking

The talking assessment will be carried out in your school by your German teacher, who will be able to help you to prepare for it well in advance. It will be recorded and marked by your teacher.

The talking assessment has two parts:

1 A presentation in German on a topic of your choice, such as:

- Meine Familie und ich
- Meine Freizeit und meine Freunde
- Meine Heimatstadt
- Meine Schule und meine Schulkarriere
- Meine Zukunftspläne
- Mein Arbeitspraktikum
- Mein Lieblingsfilm
- Mein Lieblingsbuch

The presentation should be approximately one to two minutes long, you may use notes (not sentences) and/or visual support such as a PowerPoint presentation, a picture, a photograph, an item, etc.

2 A discussion with your teacher in German

Your teacher will ask you additional questions on your presentation or may ask questions which relate to a topic derived from your presentation. The discussion should be approximately three to five minutes long.

The total mark for your Talking exam at National 5 is 30. Five out of these 30 marks will only be granted if the language you use in the conversation is natural and spontaneous.

What can you do to help you have a successful National 5 German exam?

Top tip: Do not panic!

As soon as the exam timetable is published, ask your teacher for the exact date of the German exam (usually April/May time) and mark the date and time in your diary – or on your mobile phone.

Remember that your Talking exam will be done before your Reading and Writing and Listening exams. Take this into account when you plan your revision.

Reading tips

Before you read the German texts:

- read the title/headline and ask yourself what you already know about the topic.
- look at any pictures as they support the contents of a text.
- check if the text comes with a glossary to save yourself time looking up words in the dictionary.

While you are reading the German texts:

- focus on your reading – be an active reader!
- try to figure out the main idea(s) of the text(s).
- access the meaning of a word by
  - checking the context/sentence the word is in.
  - checking if the word is similar to English (German and English have many cognates or near cognates – which are words that look and/or sound similar or even the same); many German and English words begin with the same letter or even the same two letters.
  - checking whether or not the text comes with a glossary.
  - using the dictionary.

After you have read the text and before you start answering the questions:

- read the comprehension questions carefully.
- if necessary, underline the question word to highlight exactly what kind of answer is required.
- check the tense form of the English question to make sure you use the same tense form in your answer.
- make sure that your answer has sufficient detail – compare it with the marks you can get for each answer.

Most importantly – make sure your English answers make sense and your English expression is of a good standard.

After you have answered the questions:

- allow yourself time to go over your answers.

Writing tips

Before you sit your Writing exam:

- plan the exam carefully by exploring the four predictable bullet points:
  - Make sure you know the proper conventions for your piece of writing and practise them.
  - Make a note of some vocabulary which you will need to address these bullet points and learn it. Choose five verbs, five adjectives and five nouns, for example.
  - Remember what you have practised in class when covering the topic areas you are writing about.
  - Produce a draft and show it to your teacher before the exam.

While you are sitting your Writing exam:

- read the stimulus very carefully and identify exactly what the job is that you are going to apply for. Use the dictionary for help, if necessary, and remember that jobs in German have male and female forms.

- read the two bullet points which are less predictable. Remember what you have learned in class about the topics they address.

- avoid writing very long sentences as you may lose control of structure and word order. However, try to include connectors such as und/aber/oder/denn and also some which change the word order such as weil/obwohl/dass.

- try to use different tense forms where possible, e.g. „Ich habe im letzten Jahr ein Arbeitspraktikum gemacht."/ „Ich werde das Abitur machen und Deutsch studieren."

- where possible, include opinions using German expressions such as „Ich denke, dass…"/ „Ich bin der Meinung, dass…"/ „Ich finde…"/ „Meiner Meinung nach…"

- try not to translate from English as you will be tempted to apply the English sentence structure rather than the German one – focus on the correct position of the verb in the German sentence and remember the rules of German sentence structure.

- limit yourself to 20 to 25 words per bullet point and make sure you address them all.

- focus on capitalisation of nouns and correct verb endings to achieve a high level of accuracy.

After you have finished your Writing exam:

- leave yourself enough time at the end to proofread your e-mail text.

- check that you have addressed all six bullet points.

- check your verb endings and tense forms, your adjective endings and capitalisation of nouns.

- if in doubt, use the dictionary for support.

Listening tips

Top tip: Learn your vocabulary regularly and revise systematically before the exam. Only those who recognise words will be able to understand the meaning of a spoken sentence.

Before you sit your Listening exam:

- revise vocabulary, especially verbs in their different tense forms, quantifiers (viel, wenig, die meisten), numbers and dates. Read vocabulary out loud so that you recognise acoustically what you see in front of you.

- read the title/the introduction to the listening item and ask yourself what your experience with the topic is and what you know about this topic.

- remember the close relationship between the English and the German language where many words sound very similar and use this to your benefit in listening. However, beware: "Schinken" is not "chicken"!

- read the English questions very carefully – you have one minute to study them – and underline the question words or any others which you feel might be of importance.

- remember that the questions are in chronological sequence – the answer to question (c) must be between the answers to (b) and (d) in the recording.

While you are sitting your Listening exam:

- remember that both items (monologue and dialogue) will be played three times so it is not necessary to answer any questions during the first playing.

- write your answers neatly and clearly on your question paper. If you correct your answer, make sure the marker will be able to recognise your final answer.

- if you don't understand a word which you believe to be an element of an answer – do not panic! Trust your instincts and your natural connection to German as a speaker of English and see if you can guess the meaning.

- be guided by the number of marks allocated to each question. They will tell you how much information is expected in your answer.

After your Listening exam:

- go over your answers. Make sure your English expression is as good as possible to convey meaning clearly.

- make sure you have crossed out any draft answers leaving the final answer for the marker to see.

Talking tips

Top tips:

- **Start preparing for your Talking exam in plenty of time. Practise talking regularly as practice makes perfect.**

- **Remember that your teacher will conduct the exam and that he/she will want to help you to succeed. Trust him/her.**

Before your Talking exam:

- choose a topic that you really like and have something to say about for your presentation.
- develop a piece of writing for your presentation which has a clear structure. Show this work to your teacher.
- ask your teacher to read aloud and record this text for you on your mobile phone, iPod or any other media device so that you can listen to it many times before the exam.
- turn the sentences of that text into notes. (A note is a short phrase which does not contain a verb.)
- practise your presentation by listening to the recording and reading your notes, then try it without the recording by your teacher.
- try to figure out what kind of questions your teacher might ask you in the discussion. These questions will be linked to the topic you have presented.

For example:

If you have done a presentation on your favourite film, your teacher might ask questions such as:

- „Siehst du gern fern oder gehst du lieber ins Kino?"
- „Was findest du besser – DVDs zu Hause oder einen Kinofilm mit Freunden?"
- „Hast du einen Lieblingsschauspieler/eine Lieblings-schauspielerin? Warum findest du ihn/sie gut?"
- „Welche Filme siehst du gern?"
- „Welche Fernsehsendungen siehst du gern?"

Make sure you revise and learn conventions on expressing an opinion in German, e.g. „Ich finde ...", „Ich bin der Meinung, dass...", „Meiner Meinung nach..." etc.

You should also revise and learn conventions on how to sustain a conversation – especially when you have difficulties understanding a question, e.g. „Ich habe das nicht verstanden. Bitte wiederholen Sie die Frage."/ „Ich bin nicht sicher, was das auf Deutsch/Englisch heißt."/ „Sprechen Sie bitte langsamer."

During your Talking exam:

- concentrate on your notes in your presentation. You are entitled to use them – do not do without.
- look up from your notes, keep eye contact and speak loudly and clearly to show you are confident – and to ensure a good quality of recording!
- do not panic if you are stuck – try to recover by remembering what you have worked out for your presentation.

- listen carefully to your teacher's questions and remember that you can always "steal" vocabulary from the question to make your answer.
- try to avoid very long sentences as you might lose control over the sentence structure. However, try to use connectors such as und/aber/oder/denn and also weil.
- ask for help (in German) when you need it. This will not necessarily result in a lower mark as it shows your ability to use German for clarification purposes.

After your Talking exam:

- ask your teacher if it is possible to listen to your recording and get some feedback on your performance.
- you might want to use your National 5 Talking exam as a basis for your Higher Talking exam – so keep your notes if you are thinking about taking Higher German.

In your National 5 Course Assessment, the formula to success is a sound knowledge of the level of German required, teamwork in class and with your teacher, and confidence in yourself and the skills your teacher has helped you to develop. Most importantly though, enjoy the course and the experience. Deutsch ist mega cool!

Good luck!

Remember that the rewards for passing National 5 German are well worth it! Your pass will help you get the future you want for yourself. In the exam, be confident in your own ability. If you're not sure how to answer a question, trust your instincts and just give it a go anyway. Keep calm and don't panic! GOOD LUCK!

Study Skills – what you need to know to pass exams!

General exam revision: 20 top tips

When preparing for exams, it is easy to feel unsure of where to start or how to revise. This guide to general exam revision provides a good starting place, and, as these are very general tips, they can be applied to all your exams.

1. Start revising in good time.

Don't leave revision until the last minute – this will make you panic and it will be difficult to learn. Make a revision timetable that counts down the weeks to go.

2. Work to a study plan.

Set up sessions of work spread through the weeks ahead. Make sure each session has a focus and a clear purpose. What will you study, when and why? Be realistic about what you can achieve in each session, and don't be afraid to adjust your plans as needed.

3. Make sure you know exactly when your exams are.

Get your exam dates from the SQA website and use the timetable builder tool to create your own exam schedule. You will also get a personalised timetable from your school, but this might not be until close to the exam period.

4. Make sure that you know the topics that make up each course.

Studying is easier if material is in manageable chunks – why not use the SQA topic headings or create your own from your class notes? Ask your teacher for help on this if you are not sure.

5. Break the chunks up into even smaller bits.

The small chunks should be easier to cope with. Remember that they fit together to make larger ideas. Even the process of chunking down will help!

6. Ask yourself these key questions for each course:

- Are all topics compulsory or are there choices?
- Which topics seem to come up time and time again?
- Which topics are your strongest and which are your weakest?

Use your answers to these questions to work out how much time you will need to spend revising each topic.

7. Make sure you know what to expect in the exam.

The subject-specific introduction to this book will help with this. Make sure you can answer these questions:

- How is the paper structured?
- How much time is there for each part of the exam?
- What types of question are involved? These will vary depending on the subject so read the subject-specific section carefully.

8. Past papers are a vital *revision tool!*

Use past papers to support your revision wherever possible. This book contains the answers and mark schemes too – refer to these carefully when checking your work. Using the mark scheme is useful; even if you don't manage to get all the marks available first time when you first practise, it helps you identify how to extend and develop your answers to get more marks next time – and of course, in the real exam.

9. Use study methods that work well for you.

People study and learn in different ways. Reading and looking at diagrams suits some students. Others prefer to listen and hear material – what about reading out loud or getting a friend or family member to do this for you? You could also record and play back material.

10. There are three tried and tested ways to make material stick in your long-term memory:

- Practising – e.g. rehearsal, repeating
- Organising – e.g. making drawings, lists, diagrams, tables, memory aids
- Elaborating – e.g. incorporating the material into a story or an imagined journey

11. Learn actively.

Most people prefer to learn actively – for example, making notes, highlighting, redrawing and redrafting, making up memory aids, or writing past paper answers. A good way to stay engaged and inspired is to mix and match these methods – find the combination that best suits you. This is likely to vary depending on the topic or subject.

12. Be an expert.

Be sure to have a few areas in which you feel you are an expert. This often works because at least some of them will come up, which can boost confidence.

13. Try some visual methods.

Use symbols, diagrams, charts, flashcards, post-it notes etc. Don't forget – the brain takes in chunked images more easily than loads of text.

14. Remember – practice makes perfect.

Work on difficult areas again and again. Look and read – then test yourself. You cannot do this too much.

15. Try past papers against the clock.

Practise writing answers in a set time. This is a good habit from the start but is especially important when you get closer to exam time.

16. Collaborate with friends.

Test each other and talk about the material – this can really help. Two brains are better than one! It is amazing how talking about a problem can help you solve it.

17. Know your weaknesses.

Ask your teacher for help to identify what you don't know. Try to do this as early as possible. If you are having trouble, it is probably with a difficult topic, so your teacher will already be aware of this – most students will find it tough.

18. Have your materials organised and ready.

Know what is needed for each exam:

- Do you need a calculator or a ruler?
- Should you have pencils as well as pens?
- Will you need water or paper tissues?

19. Make full use of school resources.

Find out what support is on offer:

- Are there study classes available?
- When is the library open?
- When is the best time to ask for extra help?
- Can you borrow textbooks, study guides, past papers, etc.?
- Is school open for Easter revision?

20. Keep fit and healthy!

Try to stick to a routine as much as possible, including with sleep. If you are tired, sluggish or dehydrated, it is difficult to see how concentration is even possible. Combine study with relaxation, drink plenty of water, eat sensibly, and get fresh air and exercise – all these things will help more than you could imagine. Good luck!

NATIONAL 5

2016

N5

National Qualifications 2016

Mark

X734/75/01

German Reading

WEDNESDAY, 1 JUNE
1:00 PM – 2:30 PM

Fill in these boxes and read what is printed below.

Full name of centre

Town

Forename(s)

Surname

Number of seat

Date of birth

Day   Month   Year

Scottish candidate number

Total marks — 30

Attempt ALL questions.

Write your answers clearly, in **English**, in the spaces provided in this booklet.

You may use a German dictionary.

Additional space for answers is provided at the end of this booklet. If you use this space you must clearly identify the question number you are attempting.

Use **blue** or **black** ink.

There is a separate question and answer booklet for Writing. You must complete your answer for Writing in the question and answer booklet for Writing.

Before leaving the examination room you must give this booklet to the Invigilator; if you do not, you may lose all the marks for this paper.

MARKS | DO NOT WRITE IN THIS MARGIN

Total marks — 30

Attempt ALL questions

Text 1

You read an online article explaining what citizens in Munich can do to help protect the environment.

Wie kann man als Bürger hier in München mehr für die Umwelt tun? Hier einige Tipps, wie man unseren Planeten schützen kann.

Kostenlose Zeitungen und unerwünschte Broschüren im Briefkasten bedeuten eine Verschwendung von Rohstoffen. Ein Aufkleber an der Haustür, der sagt „STOP — Bitte keine Werbung", ist eine billige und wirksame Lösung.

In München gibt es heute immer mehr Geschäfte, wo man Bio-Obst und -Gemüse kaufen kann. Hier muss man aber vorsichtig sein, denn Bio-Kiwis aus Neuseeland oder Bio-Äpfel aus Argentinien werden mit dem Flugzeug nach Deutschland transportiert und deswegen gibt es so viel Luftverschmutzung.

Wenn man etwas braucht, ist es nicht immer nötig, etwas Neues zu kaufen. Wenn man zum Beispiel einen neuen Tisch braucht, kann man einen alten Tisch auf einem Flohmarkt kaufen. Das sieht oft besser aus und ist normalerweise preiswerter.

Studenten an der Uni können sich oft gegenseitig helfen. Man kann zum Beispiel Kleider austauschen, und man kann andere Sachen wie Sportartikel teilen.

Es ist auch gut, wenn man versucht, kaputte Dinge zu reparieren. Wenn man ein Fahrrad oder eine Waschmaschine reparieren kann, ist das viel besser als etwas Neues zu kaufen. Jedes Jahr in Deutschland landen 500.000 Tonnen Elektrogeräte auf dem Schrotthaufen und das ist viel zu viel.

Questions

(a) What does the article say about junk mail? Complete the sentence.   **1**

Free newspapers and unwanted brochures are a waste of

_____ .

(b) What is a good and cheap way of stopping this junk mail?   **1**

_____

_____

MARKS | DO NOT WRITE IN THIS MARGIN

Text 1 Questions (continued)

(c) Why do you have to be careful when buying organic fruit from countries such as Argentina and New Zealand? State **two** things.   2

_____

_____

(d) What are the benefits of buying an old table instead of a brand new one? State **two** things.   2

_____

_____

(e) What can students at the university do to help? State **two** things.   2

_____

_____

(f) (i) There is a final suggestion on how to help the environment. What is this?   1

_____

_____

(ii) What statistic supports this suggestion at the end of the article? Complete the sentence.   1

500,000 tonnes of _____
land on the scrapheap each year.

[Turn over

MARKS | DO NOT WRITE IN THIS MARGIN

Text 2

You are browsing a German online magazine when the following article about an interesting school catches your eye.

Bis vor kurzem haben fast keine Schüler des Sophie Scholl Gymnasiums in München in der Schulkantine gegessen. Das Essen war wenig schmackhaft. Die Schüler gingen lieber in Fastfood-Restaurants, aber das Essen in diesen Restaurants enthält oft viel Fett.

Die Schüler haben aber eine Lösung zu diesem Problem gefunden: Sie kochen selbst jeden Tag. Alle zwei Wochen ist eine andere Klasse für das Mittagessen verantwortlich.

Der Schuldirektor findet das Projekt wichtig für die Gesundheit der Schüler. Die meisten Kinder haben ihre Essgewohnheiten geändert. Wenn sie abends nach Hause kommen, wird das Essen nicht mehr im Mikrowellenherd aufgewärmt. Die Schüler haben jetzt Lust, mit frischen Zutaten zu kochen.

Weil die Schüler so viel in der Schule machen müssen, lernen sie Verantwortung zu übernehmen. Sie lernen auch etwas über die Zusammenarbeit mit anderen und auch wie viel die Lebensmittel kosten.

Das Projekt hat viel Erfolg gehabt. Mehr Schüler essen jetzt in der Kantine. Das Schulessen ist jetzt lecker und viel gesünder. Es gibt noch einen Vorteil — die Schüler können eine zweite Portion kostenlos bekommen.

Questions

(a) What does the article say about eating habits at the Sophie Scholl Gymnasium? Complete the sentences.

2

Until recently _____ pupils ate in the school canteen.

The food was _____ .

(b) What solution have the pupils found to this problem? State **two** things.

2

_____

_____

MARKS | DO NOT WRITE IN THIS MARGIN

Text 2 Questions (continued)

(c) In what ways have eating habits for pupils changed at home? State **two** things.

2

_____

_____

(d) What have the pupils learned as a result of this project? State any **two** things.

2

_____

_____

(e) Give **two** reasons why more pupils are now eating in the canteen.

2

_____

_____

[Turn over

MARKS | DO NOT WRITE IN THIS MARGIN

Text 3

You read an article about starting your own business.

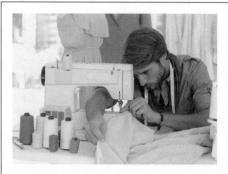

Heute wollen immer mehr Leute eine eigene Firma gründen. Das bringt sicher viele Vorteile mit sich — man kann immer das machen, was man will. Man ist selbst für Zeitmanagement verantwortlich und man hat die Chance, eigene Ideen zu entwickeln.

Manfred Schultz ist heute Inhaber einer kleinen Textilfirma. Die Idee hatte er, als er Student war: „Ich hatte begonnen, meine eigenen Kleider zu machen und ich habe sie auf dem Sonntagsmarkt in der Stadt verkauft. Sehr viele Studenten haben meine Kleider gekauft, und bald begann ich sie in der Stadt zu sehen. Das hat mich ermutigt, weiterzumachen!

Am Ende meiner Studienzeit hatte ich genug Geld für einen Gebrauchtwagen und für eine achtwöchige Reise durch ganz Italien. Später habe ich ein kleines Geschäft in meiner Heimatstadt eröffnet.

So einfach ist es aber nicht. Man muss an die Nebenkosten denken: Man braucht eine Versicherung und man muss oft eine Nähmaschine reparieren lassen.

Natürlich muss man auch mit Enttäuschungen rechnen. Viele Leute finden das schwierig. Ich hatte zum Beispiel gehofft, dass ein großes Warenhaus meine Kleider kaufen würde, aber am Ende wollten sie meine Jacken und Hemden verändern und das war für mich absolut inakzeptabel. Trotzdem bin ich immer noch zufrieden mit der Arbeit.“

Questions

(a) According to the article, what are the advantages of starting your own business? State any **two** things.

2

_____

_____

(b) (i) Where did Manfred Schultz first sell the clothes he had made?

1

_____

(ii) What things encouraged him to keep going? State **two** things.

2

_____

_____

MARKS | DO NOT WRITE IN THIS MARGIN

Text 3 Questions (continued)

(c) What did Manfred do when his studies were finished? State any **two** things.

2

_____

_____

(d) There are many additional costs involved in running a business. Give any **one** example of these.

1

_____

(e) Why did Manfred reject the chance to have his designs in a big department store?

1

_____

(f) What general view does this article give of running your own business? Tick (✓) the correct box.

1

	Tick (✓)
It's something that anyone can do.	
It's worthwhile, although there are also difficulties.	
It's just not worth all the effort.	

[END OF QUESTION PAPER]

MARKS | DO NOT WRITE IN THIS MARGIN

ADDITIONAL SPACE FOR ANSWERS

Page eight

MARKS | DO NOT WRITE IN THIS MARGIN

ADDITIONAL SPACE FOR ANSWERS

[BLANK PAGE]

DO NOT WRITE ON THIS PAGE

N5

National Qualifications 2016

Mark

X734/75/02

German Writing

WEDNESDAY, 1 JUNE
1:00 PM — 2:30 PM

Fill in these boxes and read what is printed below.

Full name of centre

Town

Forename(s)

Surname

Number of seat

Date of birth

Day   Month   Year

Scottish candidate number

Total marks — 20

Write your answer clearly, in **German**, in the space provided in this booklet.

You may use a German dictionary.

Additional space for answers is provided at the end of this booklet.

Use **blue** or **black** ink.

There is a separate question and answer booklet for Reading. You must complete your answers for Reading in the question and answer booklet for Reading.

Before leaving the examination room you must give this booklet to the Invigilator; if you do not, you may lose all the marks for this paper.

Total marks — 20

You are preparing an application for the job advertised below and you write an e-mail in **German** to the company.

Gaststube "Rheinblick"

Flußweg 3,
55422 Bacharach,
Rheinland-Pfalz

Wir suchen für unser Restaurant **einen Kellner/eine Kellnerin**.

Sind Sie fleißig, motiviert und höflich?

Haben Sie gute Englisch- und Deutschkenntnisse?

Schicken Sie Ihre Bewerbung an:

info@gaststube.rheinblick.de

To help you to write your e-mail, you have been given the following checklist.
You must include **all** of these points:

- Personal details (name, age, where you live)
- School/college/education experience until now
- Skills/interests you have which make you right for the job
- Related work experience
- Any previous links with Germany or a German-speaking country
- Any questions related to the job

Use all of the above to help you write the e-mail in **German**. The e-mail should be approximately 120—150 words. You may use a German dictionary.

MARKS | DO NOT WRITE IN THIS MARGIN

ANSWER SPACE

MARKS | DO NOT WRITE IN THIS MARGIN

ANSWER SPACE (continued)

MARKS | DO NOT WRITE IN THIS MARGIN

ANSWER SPACE (continued)

[Turn over

MARKS | DO NOT WRITE IN THIS MARGIN

ANSWER SPACE (continued)

_____

_____

_____

_____

_____

_____

_____

_____

_____

_____

_____

_____

_____

_____

_____

_____

_____

_____

_____

_____

_____

_____

_____

[END OF QUESTION PAPER]

MARKS DO NOT WRITE IN THIS MARGIN

ADDITIONAL SPACE FOR ANSWERS

ADDITIONAL SPACE FOR ANSWERS

N5

National
Qualifications
2016

Mark ☐

X734/75/03

**German
Listening**

WEDNESDAY, 1 JUNE
2:50 PM — 3:20 PM (approx)

Fill in these boxes and read what is printed below.

Full name of centre

Town

Forename(s)

Surname

Number of seat

Date of birth

| Day | Month | Year |

Scottish candidate number

Total marks — 20

Attempt ALL questions.

You will hear two items in German. **Before you hear each item, you will have one minute to study the questions**. You will hear each item three times, with an interval of one minute between playings. You will then have time to answer the questions before hearing the next item.

You may NOT use a German dictionary.

Write your answers clearly, in **English**, in the spaces provided in this booklet. Additional space for answers is provided at the end of this booklet. If you use this space you must clearly identify the question number you are attempting.

Use **blue** or **black** ink.

You are not allowed to leave the examination room until the end of the test.

Before leaving the examination room you must give this booklet to the Invigilator; if you do not, you may lose all the marks for this paper.

MARKS | DO NOT WRITE IN THIS MARGIN

Total marks — 20

Attempt ALL questions

Item 1

Evelyn Hirsch, from Hamburg, is talking about spending holidays with friends.

(a) What kind of accommodation do people choose when on holiday with friends? State any **two** things.

2

_____

_____

(b) Evelyn gives various reasons for spending holidays with friends. State any **one** of these.

1

_____

(c) Where exactly did Evelyn and her husband rent a villa last year with their friends?

1

_____

(d) Where did they find the accommodation?

1

_____

(e) What does Evelyn enjoy doing on holiday? State any **two** things.

2

_____

_____

(f) What is Evelyn's personal view on holidays with friends? Tick (✓) the correct statement.

1

	Tick (✓)
It's the only way to get the most out of a holiday.	
She's tried it and won't do it again.	
She's looking forward to doing it again.	

MARKS | DO NOT WRITE IN THIS MARGIN

Item 2

Evelyn and her husband Rolf are discussing their plans for this year's holiday.

(a) Why does Rolf want to go on holiday to Italy? Complete the following sentence.

1

Rolf wants to go to Italy because _____ recommended it to him.

(b) What reasons does Evelyn give for wanting to stay in Germany for the holidays? State any **two**.

2

_____

_____

(c) Why does Rolf not want to spend a holiday in a town? Give any **one** reason.

1

_____

(d) Where in Germany does Evelyn suggest that they could spend this year's holiday?

1

_____

(e) Why does Rolf not want to go there? State any **one** reason.

1

_____

(f) Why does Rolf suggest a holiday in Austria? Complete the following sentences.

2

Rolf wants to go to Austria because _____ .

It's beautiful and _____ .

(g) What puts Evelyn off going to Austria this year? State any **one** thing.

1

_____

(h) Rolf says Edinburgh is a wonderful place. Why else does he want to go there?

1

_____

[Turn over

Page three

MARKS | DO NOT WRITE IN THIS MARGIN

Item 2 (continued)

(i)   Where do they finally decide to spend this year's holiday?   **1**

_____

(j)   What job will they do while on holiday?   **1**

_____

[END OF QUESTION PAPER]

MARKS | DO NOT WRITE IN THIS MARGIN

ADDITIONAL SPACE FOR ANSWERS

MARKS | DO NOT WRITE IN THIS MARGIN

ADDITIONAL SPACE FOR ANSWERS

National
Qualifications
2016

X734/75/13

German
Listening Transcript

WEDNESDAY, 1 JUNE
2:50 PM — 3:20 PM (approx)

This paper must not be seen by any candidate.

The material overleaf is provided for use in an emergency only (eg the recording or equipment proving faulty) or where permission has been given in advance by SQA for the material to be read to candidates with additional support needs. The material must be read exactly as printed.

> **Instructions to reader(s):**
>
> For each item, read the English once, then read the German **three times**, with an interval of 1 minute between the three playings. On completion of the third reading, pause for the length of time indicated in brackets after the item, to allow the candidates to write their answers.
>
> Where special arrangements have been agreed in advance to allow the reading of the material, those sections marked **(f)** should be read by a female speaker and those marked **(m)** by a male; those sections marked **(t)** should be read by the teacher.

(t)   Item Number One

Evelyn Hirsch, from Hamburg, is talking about spending holidays with friends.

You now have one minute to study the questions for Item Number One.

(f)   Sehr viele Deutsche fahren jedes Jahr in den Urlaub und Millionen von uns verbringen gern Ferien mit Freunden. Wir mieten ein Strandhaus auf Korfu, eine Ferienwohnung in Spanien oder wir verbringen Zeit in einem Wohnwagen in den Alpen.

Ja, solche Ferien mit Freunden sind sehr beliebt und es gibt viele Gründe dafür: Man kann zusammenwohnen und die Arbeit teilen, zum Beispiel das Kochen und Abwaschen. Es ist viel billiger als im Hotel und viele Leute haben Freunde, die vielleicht eine andere Sprache sprechen können. Für uns war es aber ganz anders.

Mein Mann und ich sind letztes Jahr nach Südfrankreich gefahren und wir haben eine Ferienvilla mit unseren Freunden Lars und Annette geteilt. Die Villa haben wir in einer Ferienbroschüre gefunden. Von Anfang an war es eine absolute Katastrophe.

Im Urlaub liege ich sehr gern in der Sonne, schwimme im Meer oder ich gehe gern ins große Einkaufszentrum in der nächsten Stadt. Mein Mann Rolf verbringt am liebsten Zeit in der Kunstgalerie. Letztes Jahr konnten wir das nicht machen, weil unsere Freunde auch da waren. Nächstes Jahr fahren wir allein in den Urlaub.

(2 minutes)

(t) Item Number Two

Evelyn and her husband Rolf are discussing their plans for this year's holiday.

You now have one minute to study the questions for Item Number Two.

(m) Ich möchte dieses Jahr die Ferien in Italien verbringen. Meine Chefin war letztes Jahr da und sie meint, dass das Land sehr schön sei, und die Leute sehr freundlich.

(f) Schon gut Rolf, aber Ferien im Ausland sind nicht immer was für mich. Man kann auch hier in Deutschland bleiben und gute Ferien haben. Man kann überall mit dem Auto hinfahren und man kann das Land besser kennen lernen.

(m) Ich will unter keinen Umständen meine Ferien in einer Stadt verbringen. Im Urlaub will ich Hektik und Stress vergessen. Für mich ist die Ruhe sehr wichtig.

(f) Ja, vielleicht hast du Recht. Wie wär's mit einem kleinen Ferienhaus an der Nordseeküste?

(m) Nee. Das ist auch keine gute Idee. Du weißt ja, dass das Wetter da oft furchtbar ist. Ich war letztes Jahr in Norddeutschland und es hat die ganze Zeit geregnet.

(f) Ja gut, dann ist ein Urlaub in der Stadt perfekt, weil es immer viel zu tun gibt, auch wenn das Wetter nicht gut ist.

(m) Wir könnten einen Kompromiss finden. Warum fahren wir nicht nach Österreich? Es ist nicht zu weit weg, die Landschaft ist wunderschön, und so teuer ist es auch nicht. Was meinst du?

(f) Österreich ist sicher ein sehr schönes Land, aber ich will da nicht hinfahren. Ich war vor zwei Jahren mit meiner Schwester da. Es war ganz gut, aber ich will etwas Neues erleben. Hast du vergessen?

(m) Wir könnten vielleicht eine Woche in Schottland verbringen. Edinburg soll eine wunderbare Stadt sein, und die Einkaufsmöglichkeiten sind super.

(f) Aber Rolf, du wolltest doch keine Stadtferien. Edinburg ist ja die Hauptstadt von Schottland und es gibt sicher viele Touristen im Sommer da.

(m) Mmm, vielleicht hast du Recht Evelyn. Ich glaube, wir werden dieses Jahr zu Hause bleiben. Wir können dadurch Geld sparen und wir müssen endlich die Zeit finden, die Garage aufzuräumen.

(2 minutes)

(t) End of test.

Now look over your answers.

[END OF TRANSCRIPT]

[BLANK PAGE]

DO NOT WRITE ON THIS PAGE

NATIONAL 5

2017

N5

National Qualifications 2017

Mark

X734/75/01

German Reading

FRIDAY, 2 JUNE
1:00 PM – 2:30 PM

Fill in these boxes and read what is printed below.

Full name of centre

Town

Forename(s)

Surname

Number of seat

Date of birth

Day   Month   Year

Scottish candidate number

Total marks — 30

Attempt ALL questions.

Write your answers clearly, in **English**, in the spaces provided in this booklet.

You may use a German dictionary.

Additional space for answers is provided at the end of this booklet. If you use this space you must clearly identify the question number you are attempting.

Use **blue** or **black** ink.

There is a separate question and answer booklet for Writing. You must complete your answer for Writing in the question and answer booklet for Writing.

Before leaving the examination room you must give both booklets to the Invigilator; if you do not, you may lose all the marks for this paper.

MARKS | DO NOT WRITE IN THIS MARGIN

Total marks — 30

Attempt ALL questions

Text 1

You read an article about a young woman who has learned to fly a plane.

Diese starke Frau kennt keine Grenzen

Jessica Cox ist der erste Mensch ohne Arme, der den Pilotenschein gemacht hat. Mit einem strahlenden Lächeln steigt Jessica nach dem Flug aus dem Flieger. ,,Fliegen ist das beste Gefühl der Welt", schwärmt sie. Das Besondere daran — Jessica wurde ohne Arme geboren. Sie steuert das Flugzeug mit den Füßen.

Nach dreijähriger Ausbildung und entgegen allen Erwartungen hat Jessica ihren Pilotenschein endlich bekommen. Als Jessica ihren Eltern am Anfang gesagt hat, dass sie Pilotin werden möchte, haben sie sich Sorgen gemacht und Bedenken gehegt. Trotzdem haben sie Jessica unterstützt, um die Herausforderungen zu überwinden.

Jessica hat jetzt viel mehr Zeit für sich nach dem Ende ihrer Ausbildung und nutzt ihre Freizeit völlig aus. Jede Woche geht sie mit Freunden klettern. Außerdem ist sie seit mehreren Jahren Mitglied im Segelverein und verbringt jedes zweite Wochenende am Meer.

Jessica ist für alle jungen Leute ein tolles Vorbild und sie will jetzt andere Teenager ermutigen, ihre Wünsche und Träume zu erfüllen. Sie hat im Fernsehen viele Interviews gegeben und in ihrer alten Schule über ihre Abenteuer gesprochen. Sie hat auch kostenlose Flüge für behinderte Kinder organisiert. Damit wollte sie ihnen zeigen, dass alles möglich ist.

,,Man sollte nie aufgeben. Ich habe gelernt, meinen Traum zu leben und nicht mein Leben zu träumen. Das kann jeder auch," meint Jessica.

Questions

(a) In what way does Jessica describe flying in the first paragraph?

1

_____

(b) What makes Jessica's achievement unique? State **two** things.

2

_____

_____

MARKS | DO NOT WRITE IN THIS MARGIN

Text 1 Questions (continued)

(c) What was her parents' reaction when she first told them she wanted to be a pilot? State any **two** things.

2

_____

_____

(d) In what ways does Jessica spend her free time? State any **two** things.

2

_____

_____

(e) What has Jessica done to encourage other teenagers to fulfil their dreams? State any **two** things.

2

_____

_____

(f) Jessica gives advice at the end of the article. What advice does she give? State any **one** thing.

1

_____

[Turn over

Text 2

You read an article about outdoor learning at a primary school near Berlin.

Einmal im Monat haben die Schüler der Beethoven-Grundschule draußen in dem benachbarten Wald Unterricht.

Maria Schneider, eine Lehrerin der Schule, behauptet, dass der Unterricht draußen in der Natur viele Vorteile mit sich bringt. ,,Die Schüler lernen die örtliche Umgebung und die Natur besser kennen. Sie benutzen alle ihre Sinne, um über den natürlichen Lebensraum von Insekten, Pflanzen und Tieren zu lernen. Outdoor-Lernen ist ein sehr wichtiges Erlebnis für alle Kinder."

Der zwölfjährige Thorsten Bachmann mag es sehr, im Freien zu lernen. ,,Ich hasse es, wenn man im Klassenraum sitzen muss, während draußen die Sonne scheint. Ich arbeite gern mit meinen Freunden, um Rätsel zusammen zu lösen und Spiele zusammen zu spielen. Am meisten Spaß macht es, etwas über Tiere zu lernen. Letzte Woche entdeckten wir die Muster in der Natur: die Blütenblätter, die Adern eines Blattes und die Rinde eines Baumes."

Outdoor-Lernen ist auch gut für die Gesundheit. Draußen sein bedeutet, dass die Schüler Zeit an der frischen Luft verbringen dürfen, sich regelmäßig bewegen und ihre Immunsysteme stärken. Die vermehrte Menge an Sauerstoff im Körper hilft den Schülern, sich besser konzentrieren zu können.

Jedoch muss der Unterricht manchmal kurzfristig abgesagt werden, weil das Wetter nicht immer zuverlässig ist.

Questions

(a) Where do the pupils at the *Beethoven-Grundschule* have their lessons once a month?   **1**

_____

(b) Maria Schneider is a teacher at the school. What advantages of outdoor learning does she mention? State any **two** things.   **2**

_____

_____

MARKS | DO NOT WRITE IN THIS MARGIN

Text 2 Questions (continued)

(c) Why does Thorsten Bachmann enjoy learning outdoors? State any **two** things.

2

_____

_____

(d) What patterns in nature did he discover last week? State any **two** things.

2

_____

_____

(e) In what ways is outdoor learning good for pupils' health? State any **two** things.

2

_____

_____

(f) Why do the lessons sometimes need to be cancelled at short notice? Complete the sentence:

The lessons sometimes need to be cancelled at short notice because the

weather is _____ .

1

[Turn over

MARKS DO NOT WRITE IN THIS MARGIN

Text 3

You read an article online about the advantages of taking a gap year after school.

Letztes Jahr haben fast ein Drittel der deutschen Schulabsolventen zwischen Schule und Studium oder Ausbildung ein Brückenjahr genommen. Das Brückenjahr ermöglicht vielen Jugendlichen, etwas Ungewöhnliches und Lohnendes zu unternehmen, Arbeitserfahrung zu sammeln, die Welt zu bereisen und neue Länder und Kulturen zu entdecken.

Viele Universitäten und Berufsschulen ermutigen Schulabsolventen, sich ein Jahr frei zu nehmen. Sie sind sich einig, dass dieses Jahr sich positiv auf die neuen Studenten auswirkt, weil sie sich dadurch besser auf die neuen Herausforderungen an der Uni vorbereiten. Max Weber, ein Dozent an der Uni Bonn, berichtet, dass „ein Brückenjahr eine wertvolle Erfahrung für die meisten Studenten ist. Die Studenten sind normalerweise fokussierter, haben nützliche Lebenserfahrungen und entwickeln einen starken Charakter. Gute Noten in der Schule sind nicht mehr genug, um an der Uni erfolgreich zu sein."

Außerdem ist die Erfahrung aus dem Brückenjahr sehr hilfreich, wenn man sich für einen Job bewirbt. Arbeitgeber suchen immer nach Kandidaten mit interessanten Lebensläufen und Bewerbungen. Die Erfahrung aus dem Brückenjahr kann in Vorstellungsgesprächen sehr nützlich sein. Arbeitgeber wollen, dass man echte Beispiele nennt, wie:

- wann man Initiative gezeigt hat
- wann man unter Druck gearbeitet hat
- wann man in einem Team gearbeitet hat
- wann man Verantwortung übernommen hat.

Ein Brückenjahr ermöglicht es den Bewerbern, aus der Masse herauszuragen* und es schafft ihnen einen Vorsprung in allen Bewerbungsgesprächen.

*herausragen — to stand out

Questions

(a) How many German school leavers took a gap year last year?

1

MARKS | DO NOT WRITE IN THIS MARGIN

Text 3 Questions (continued)

(b) Why do many German school leavers take a gap year? State any **two** things.

2

_____

_____

(c) Universities and colleges encourage school leavers to take a gap year. Why is this? Complete the following sentence:

A gap year is positive for new students, as they are better prepared for

the _____ at university.

1

(d) What does Max Weber say about students who have taken a gap year? State any **two** things.

2

_____

_____

(e) Gap year experience is also beneficial when applying for a job. What are employers always looking for?

1

_____

(f) Employers want candidates to provide real examples in interviews. What types of examples are they looking for? State any **three** things.

3

_____

_____

_____

[END OF QUESTION PAPER]

ADDITIONAL SPACE FOR ANSWERS

MARKS | DO NOT WRITE IN THIS MARGIN

ADDITIONAL SPACE FOR ANSWERS

[BLANK PAGE]

DO NOT WRITE ON THIS PAGE

N5

National Qualifications 2017

Mark ☐

X734/75/02

German Writing

FRIDAY, 2 JUNE
1:00 PM — 2:30 PM

Fill in these boxes and read what is printed below.

Full name of centre

Town

Forename(s)

Surname

Number of seat

Date of birth
Day   Month   Year

Scottish candidate number

Total marks — 20

Write your answer clearly, in **German**, in the space provided in this booklet.

You may use a German dictionary.

Additional space for answers is provided at the end of this booklet.

Use **blue** or **black** ink.

There is a separate question and answer booklet for Reading. You must complete your answers for Reading in the question and answer booklet for Reading.

Before leaving the examination room you must give both booklets to the Invigilator; if you do not, you may lose all the marks for this paper.

Total marks — 20

You are preparing an application for the job advertised below and you write an e-mail in **German** to the company.

Hotel Seepark
GERHART-HAUPTMANN-STRAßE — 79110 FREIBURG

Wir suchen für unser Seepark Hotel ab sofort **einen Rezeptionist/eine Rezeptionistin.**

Ihr Profil:

Sie haben

- sehr gute Deutsch- und Englischkenntnisse
- Berufserfahrung in vergleichbarer Position/an der Rezeption

Sie sind

- organisiert, freundlich und stressresistent
- flexibel und zuverlässig

Für weitere Information können Sie uns unter info@hotelseepark.de kontaktieren.

To help you to write your e-mail, you have been given the following checklist.

You must include **all** of these points:

- Personal details (name, age, where you live)
- School/college/education experience until now
- Skills/interests you have which make you right for the job
- Related work experience
- Your reason for wanting to work in Germany
- What you plan to do when you leave school/college

Use all of the above to help you write the e-mail in **German**. The e-mail should be approximately 120—150 words. You may use a German dictionary.

MARKS

ANSWER SPACE

ANSWER SPACE (continued)

ANSWER SPACE (continued)

ANSWER SPACE (continued)

[END OF QUESTION PAPER]

MARKS | DO NOT WRITE IN THIS MARGIN

ADDITIONAL SPACE FOR ANSWERS

ADDITIONAL SPACE FOR ANSWERS

N5

National Qualifications 2017

Mark ☐

X734/75/03

German Listening

FRIDAY, 2 JUNE
2:50 PM – 3:20 PM (approx)

Fill in these boxes and read what is printed below.

Full name of centre

Town

Forename(s)

Surname

Number of seat

Date of birth

Day	Month	Year	Scottish candidate number

Total marks — 20

Attempt ALL questions.

You will hear two items in German. **Before you hear each item, you will have one minute to study the questions.** You will hear each item three times, with an interval of one minute between playings. You will then have time to answer the questions before hearing the next item.

You may NOT use a German dictionary.

Write your answers clearly, in **English**, in the spaces provided in this booklet. Additional space for answers is provided at the end of this booklet. If you use this space you must clearly identify the question number you are attempting.

Use **blue** or **black** ink.

You are not allowed to leave the examination room until the end of the test.

Before leaving the examination room you must give this booklet to the Invigilator; if you do not, you may lose all the marks for this paper.

SQA

MARKS | DO NOT WRITE IN THIS MARGIN

Total marks — 20

Attempt ALL questions

Item 1

Max talks about where he lives.

(a) Where does Max live? Tick (✓) the correct box.   1

	Tick (✓)
In the city centre.	
On a farm.	
In a village.	

(b) Why is his home important to him?   1

_____

_____

(c) What does Max say about where he lives? State any **two** things.   2

_____

_____

(d) Max says there are disadvantages of where he lives. What problems does he mention? State **two** things.   2

_____

_____

(e) Why is Max unhappy about asking his parents to take him places by car? State **one** thing.   1

_____

(f) Max meets his friends in the town at the weekend. What do they do? State **two** things.   1

_____

_____

MARKS | DO NOT WRITE IN THIS MARGIN

Item 2

Hannah and Max discuss the advantages and disadvantages of life in the town and in the country.

(a) How long has Hannah lived in Munich?

1

_____

(b) Where exactly did Hannah live before she moved to Munich?

1

_____

_____

(c) What did Hannah used to do in her free time? State any **two** things.

2

_____

_____

(d) What does Hannah miss about her old life? State any **two** things.

2

_____

_____

(e) What disadvantages of life in the country does she mention? State any **one** thing.

1

_____

_____

(f) Why does Hannah like living in Munich? State any **two** things.

2

_____

_____

(g) What benefit did Munich have for her mother?

1

_____

_____

[Turn over

MARKS | DO NOT WRITE IN THIS MARGIN

Item 2 (continued)

(h) Complete the sentence.

2

Hannah wants to live _____ when she is older because

there are more _____.

[END OF QUESTION PAPER]

ADDITIONAL SPACE FOR ANSWERS

MARKS | DO NOT WRITE IN THIS MARGIN

MARKS

ADDITIONAL SPACE FOR ANSWERS

National Qualifications 2017

X734/75/13

German
Listening Transcript

FRIDAY, 2 JUNE

2:50 PM — 3:20 PM (approx)

This paper must not be seen by any candidate.

The material overleaf is provided for use in an emergency only (eg the recording or equipment proving faulty) or where permission has been given in advance by SQA for the material to be read to candidates with additional support needs. The material must be read exactly as printed.

Instructions to reader(s):

For each item, read the English **once**, then read the German **three times**, with an interval of 1 minute between the three readings. On completion of the third reading, pause for the length of time indicated in brackets after the item, to allow the candidates to write their answers.

Where special arrangements have been agreed in advance to allow the reading of the material, those sections marked **(f)** should be read by a female speaker and those marked **(m)** by a male; those sections marked **(t)** should be read by the teacher.

(t)   Item Number One

Max talks about where he lives.

You now have one minute to study the questions for Item Number One.

(m) Ich wohne auf einem Bauernhof in der Nähe von Heidelberg. Unser Bauernhof ist ein Weingut auf dem wir viele Trauben und auch Gemüse haben.

Es ist mir sehr wichtig, hier zu wohnen und zu arbeiten, denn mein Vater und mein Großvater haben auch hier gewohnt und gearbeitet.

Auf dem Bauernhof ist es sehr ruhig und sauber. Es ist wirklich wunderschön und wir haben eine tolle Aussicht auf den Fluss.

Trotzdem gibt es Nachteile. Das Problem ist, es kann abends einsam sein, weil meine Freunde alle weit weg wohnen. Ich sehe meine Freunde in der Schule, aber auf dem Land sind die Verkehrsverbindungen schlecht. Ich muss immer meine Eltern fragen, ob sie mich mit dem Auto fahren können. Das gefällt mir nicht, weil ich selbstständig sein möchte.

Aber am Wochenende gehe ich oft mit meinen Freunden in die Stadt. Wir gehen gerne ins Kino oder in den Jugendklub. Die Stadt hat viele Unterhaltungsmöglichkeiten für Jugendliche, aber ich kann mir nicht vorstellen, in der Stadt zu wohnen. Dort ist es mir zu laut und es gibt zu viele Leute. Obwohl es Nachteile gibt, liebe ich das Leben auf dem Bauernhof.

(2 minutes)

(t) **Item Number Two**

Hannah and Max discuss the advantages and disadvantages of life in the town and in the country.

You now have one minute to study the questions for Item Number Two.

(m) Seit wann wohnst du in München, Hannah?

(f) Ich wohne seit drei Jahren hier.

(m) Und wo hast du früher gewohnt?

(f) Früher habe ich in einem Dorf an der Grenze zu Österreich gewohnt. Dort war ich bei meinem Vater, weil meine Eltern nicht mehr zusammen waren. Aber mein Vater hat wieder geheiratet und ich mag meine Stiefmutter nicht, deswegen lebe ich jetzt gemeinsam mit meiner Mutter in München.

(m) Wie war das Leben in einem kleinen Dorf?

(f) Ich war jung und es war ganz okay. Es gab einige kleine Geschäfte und ein Eiscafé, aber nichts Besonderes. Ich hatte ein paar Freunde im Dorf und wir hatten Spaß.

(m) Was hast du in deiner Freizeit gemacht?

(f) Ich habe meine Freunde besucht und wir haben zusammen Sport getrieben, ferngesehen und geplaudert. Manchmal gab es im Sommer Grillpartys bei Freunden. Wir haben viel gelacht und danach im Freien gezeltet.

(m) Vermisst du das Leben auf dem Land?

(f) Ja. Ich vermisse meine Freunde und auch die frische Luft. Es ist sicherer auf dem Land und das Leben ist nicht so hektisch.

(m) Gibt es deiner Meinung nach auch Nachteile, wenn man auf dem Land wohnt?

(f) Klar gibt es Nachteile. Es gibt keine Busse und es ist nicht viel los für junge Leute.

(m) Wie findest du dein Leben hier in einer Großstadt?

(f) Ich mag München. Es hat alles, was man braucht und es ist nie langweilig. Ich kann zum Beispiel oft ins Kino gehen und es gibt große Einkaufszentren, wo man gut einkaufen kann. Meine Mutter hat ziemlich schnell eine Arbeit in München gefunden, und auf dem Land ist das nicht so einfach.

(m) Und wo willst du später wohnen?

(f) Bestimmt in einer großen Stadt, da es mehr Freizeitmöglichkeiten gibt.

(2 minutes)

(t) **End of test.**

Now look over your answers.

[END OF TRANSCRIPT]

[BLANK PAGE]

DO NOT WRITE ON THIS PAGE

NATIONAL 5

2018

N5

National
Qualifications
2018

Mark

X834/75/01

German Reading

MONDAY, 4 JUNE

1:00 PM – 2:30 PM

Fill in these boxes and read what is printed below.

Full name of centre

Town

Forename(s)

Surname

Number of seat

Date of birth

Day   Month   Year   Scottish candidate number

Total marks — 30

Attempt ALL questions.

Write your answers clearly, in **English**, in the spaces provided in this booklet.

You may use a German dictionary.

Additional space for answers is provided at the end of this booklet. If you use this space you must clearly identify the question number you are attempting.

Use **blue** or **black** ink.

There is a separate question and answer booklet for Writing. You must complete your answer for Writing in the question and answer booklet for Writing.

Before leaving the examination room you must give both booklets to the Invigilator; if you do not, you may lose all the marks for this paper.

MARKS | DO NOT WRITE IN THIS MARGIN

Total marks — 30

Attempt ALL questions

Text 1

In this item, Karsten is writing about his job on a farm.

Ich arbeite seit vier Jahren auf dem Bauernhof. Die Arbeit hier ist ideal — ich kann mir gar nicht vorstellen, in einer Stadt zu arbeiten, weil es dort viel zu viel Lärm und Verkehr gibt.

Natürlich ist der Job körperlich anstrengend. Man verdient nicht besonders gut und oft ist es unglaublich dreckig, besonders wenn man mit Tieren wie Kühen und Schafen umgeht. Trotzdem muss ich zugeben, dass meine Arbeit mir Spaß macht.

Einmal in der Woche gehe ich in die Berufsschule, wo wir herausfinden, wie man die Theorie und Praxis der Landwirtschaft kombiniert. Wir lernen auch viel über die verschiedenen Aspekte des Lebens auf einem Bauernhof. In der Zukunft hoffe ich, meinen eigenen Bauernhof zu besitzen und dafür ist diese Erfahrung so wertvoll.

Die Aussichten für Bauern in Deutschland, vor allem Kleinbauern, sind nicht so rosig. Milch- und Fleischprodukte bringen keinen großen Gewinn mehr, und viele Kleinbauern bekommen weniger finanzielle Hilfe von der Regierung.

Weitere Probleme in der Landwirtschaft: Für die Maschinen auf dem Bauernhof muss man so viel ausgeben und sie müssen ständig repariert werden.

Stimmt, Bauer sein hat viele Nachteile. Ich weiß, dass es Probleme gibt, aber es ist jedoch mein Traumjob.

Questions

(a) Karsten cannot see himself ever working in a town. Why is this? Give **two** reasons.

1

_____

_____

MARKS | DO NOT WRITE IN THIS MARGIN

Text 1 questions (continued)

(b) Karsten talks about the negative aspects of his work. Complete the following sentences.   **2**

Obviously the work is _____ .

You don't earn that much and it is often _____

_____ .

(c) Karsten talks about going to college once a week.

   (i) What **exactly** does he learn when he goes to college? State **two** things.   **2**

_____

_____

_____

   (ii) Why will this help him with his plans for the future?   **1**

_____

(d) What factors are making life harder for farmers, especially small farmers? State **two** things.   **2**

_____

_____

_____

(e) Why is farm machinery a problem? State **two** things.   **2**

_____

_____

[Turn over

MARKS | DO NOT WRITE IN THIS MARGIN

Text 2

You are doing some research for an art project when you come across the following article about graffiti art in Berlin.

Graffiti in Berlin

Berlin ist die Graffiti-Hauptstadt von Europa. Graffiti-Künstler aus aller Welt kommen nach Berlin, um ihre Kreativität zu entwickeln. Die meisten Graffiti-Sprayer sind zwischen 13 und 21 Jahre alt und für sie ist Graffiti ein wichtiger Teil der Jugendkultur. Sie malen Graffiti auf Züge und Unterführungen, aber am liebsten malen sie in U-Bahnstationen.

Soll Berlin stolz auf seine Graffitis sein? Diese Frage wird oft kontrovers diskutiert. Einige Leute finden die Graffitis toll. Ihrer Meinung nach sind Graffitis echte Kunstwerke und machen die langweiligen grauen Mauern in der Hauptstadt bunter und lebendiger. Andere Berliner dagegen finden, dass Graffitis aggressiv wirken und die Gebäude der Stadt verderben.

Das Sprayen ist illegal, weil die Beseitigung von Graffiti in Berlin jedes Jahr 35 bis 50 Millionen Euro kostet. Aber die Stadt erlaubt einige Graffiti-Wände, weil sie ein Tourismusmagnet sind. Berlin hat neulich 2,2 Millionen Euro für die Restaurierung von Mauermalereien an der East-Side-Gallery, einem Teil der Berliner Mauer, bezahlt.

Die East-Side-Gallery ist bei Touristen sehr beliebt, weil sie ein internationales Symbol der Freiheit ist. Diese Touristen können mehr als hundert Bilder von Künstlern aus der ganzen Welt sehen.

Questions

(a) Berlin is the graffiti capital of Europe. Complete the following sentence. **1**

Graffiti artists come to Berlin to _____ .

(b) What does graffiti mean to the graffiti artists themselves? **1**

_____

MARKS | DO NOT WRITE IN THIS MARGIN

Text 2 questions (continued)

(c) Where do they **most** like to spray graffiti? Tick (✓) the correct box. **1**

	Tick (✓)
On trains	
In underground stations	
On underpasses	

(d) Graffiti is a controversial topic in Berlin.

　　(i) Why do some people think that the graffiti in Berlin is great? State **two** things. **2**

　　　_____

　　　_____

　　(ii) Why do other Berliners object to graffiti? State any **one** thing. **1**

　　　_____

　　　_____

(e) Why is spray painting illegal? **1**

　_____

　_____

(f) What has Berlin recently spent 2.2 million euros on? **1**

　_____

(g) Why is the East-Side-Gallery popular with tourists? State **two** things. **2**

　_____

　_____

　_____

[Turn over

MARKS | DO NOT WRITE IN THIS MARGIN

Text 3

This passage tells of a German school where parents spend a week with their children.

Im Mai diesen Jahres haben viele Eltern eine Woche mit ihren Kindern im Adenauer-Gymnasium in Frankfurt verbracht. Die Idee für eine Elternwoche hatte die neue Schuldirektorin Sandra Götz, als sie eine Partnerschule in Brasilien besucht hat.

Im Großen und Ganzen war diese Elternwoche ein riesiger Erfolg: „Ich war wirklich erstaunt," sagte Frau Götz. „Die meisten Kinder in meiner Schule waren froh, ihre Eltern in der Schule zu haben. Sie wollten zeigen, was sie im Unterricht gemacht und gelernt hatten."

Es ist aber nicht einfach, eine Elternwoche zu organisieren. Als Erstes sind nicht alle Kinder so begeistert, ihre Eltern in der Schule zu sehen. Dann braucht jeder Erwachsene eine Bescheinigung von der Polizei, bevor er/sie Zeit in der Schule verbringen darf. Das kann man nicht an einem Tag organisieren.

Frau Götz ist aber überzeugt, dass die Kinder von der Elternwoche profitiert haben: „Ein paar Eltern, die bei Firmen in der Stadt arbeiten, haben mit den Schülern über die Arbeitswelt gesprochen. Jetzt haben wir ein Netzwerk von guten Kontakten mit Firmen und Arbeitgebern in der Stadt."

Und die Eltern? Was sagen sie dazu?

- „Junge Menschen lernen heute mehr über die Welt, als wir damals gelernt haben"

- „Meine Kinder haben Spaß an der Zusammenarbeit mit ihren Klassenkameraden."

- „Die Beziehung zwischen Lehrer und Klasse ist sehr locker und entspannt."

Questions

(a) Sandra Götz introduced the idea of a parents' week.

   (i) Who is Sandra Götz? **1**

   _____

   (ii) Where **exactly** did she get the idea for a parents' week? **1**

   _____

MARKS | DO NOT WRITE IN THIS MARGIN

Text 3 questions (continued)

(b) How did most of the children feel about the week?

2

_____

_____

(c) What makes it difficult to set up a parents' week in school? State **two** things.

2

_____

_____

(d) In what ways does Sandra Götz feel that the pupils have benefited from the parents' week? State **two** things.

2

_____

_____

(e) What have the parents learned about their children's experience of school? State **two** things.

2

_____

_____

[END OF QUESTION PAPER]

ADDITIONAL SPACE FOR ANSWERS

MARKS | DO NOT WRITE IN THIS MARGIN

ADDITIONAL SPACE FOR ANSWERS

[BLANK PAGE]

DO NOT WRITE ON THIS PAGE

N5

National Qualifications 2018

Mark

X834/75/02

German Writing

MONDAY, 4 JUNE
1:00 PM – 2:30 PM

Fill in these boxes and read what is printed below.

Full name of centre

Town

Forename(s)

Surname

Number of seat

Date of birth

Day	Month	Year	Scottish candidate number

Total marks — 20

Write your answer clearly, in **German**, in the space provided in this booklet.

You may use a German dictionary.

Additional space for answers is provided at the end of this booklet.

Use **blue** or **black** ink.

There is a separate question and answer booklet for Reading. You must complete your answers for Reading in the question and answer booklet for Reading.

Before leaving the examination room you must give both booklets to the Invigilator; if you do not, you may lose all the marks for this paper.

NATIONAL 5 GERMAN 82 SQA EXAM PAPER 2018

MARKS | DO NOT WRITE IN THIS MARGIN

Total marks — 20

You are preparing an application for the job advertised below and you write an e-mail in **German** to the employer.

Visit Berlin

Hauptfremdenverkehrsamt
Kurfürstendamm 154
Berlin

sucht
Mitarbeiter/-innen

Arbeiten Sie gern mit Touristen und in einem Team?
Sprechen Sie eine (oder mehrere) Fremdsprache(n)?
Sind Sie hilfsbereit, geduldig und freundlich?
Interessieren Sie sich für Kultur und Geschichte?

Wir freuen uns auf Ihre Bewerbung
Schicken Sie uns eine E-mail an:

personalabteilung@visitberlin.de

To help you to write your e-mail, you have been given the following checklist.
You must include **all** of these points:

- Personal details (name, age, where you live)
- School/college/education experience until now
- Skills/interests you have which make you right for the job
- Related work experience
- Any previous links with Germany or a German-speaking country
- Details of any career/job plans you have for the future

Use all of the above to help you write the e-mail in **German**. The e-mail should be approximately 120—150 words. You may use a German dictionary.

ANSWER SPACE

ANSWER SPACE (continued)

MARKS | DO NOT WRITE IN THIS MARGIN

ANSWER SPACE (continued)

ANSWER SPACE (continued)

[END OF QUESTION PAPER]

MARKS DO NOT WRITE IN THIS MARGIN

ADDITIONAL SPACE FOR ANSWERS

ADDITIONAL SPACE FOR ANSWERS

N5

National Qualifications 2018

Mark ☐

X834/75/03

German Listening

MONDAY, 4 JUNE

2:50 PM – 3:20 PM (approx)

Fill in these boxes and read what is printed below.

Full name of centre

Town

Forename(s)

Surname

Number of seat

Date of birth

Day	Month	Year	Scottish candidate number

Total marks — 20

Attempt ALL questions.

You will hear two items in German. **Before you hear each item, you will have one minute to study the questions.** You will hear each item three times, with an interval of one minute between playings. You will then have time to answer the questions before hearing the next item.

You may NOT use a German dictionary.

Write your answers clearly, in **English**, in the spaces provided in this booklet. Additional space for answers is provided at the end of this booklet. If you use this space you must clearly identify the question number you are attempting.

Use **blue** or **black** ink.

You are not allowed to leave the examination room until the end of the test.

Before leaving the examination room you must give this booklet to the Invigilator; if you do not, you may lose all the marks for this paper.

MARKS | DO NOT WRITE IN THIS MARGIN

Total marks — 20

Attempt ALL questions

Item 1

You hear a radio report with Eva, an aid worker.

(a) Eva talks about her job as an aid worker. What does she say? Give **one** detail.

1

_____

(b) Where does her aid agency work? Tick (✓) the correct answer.

1

	Tick (✓)
All over the world	
In war zones	

(c) In what ways do Eva and her aid agency help? Complete the sentence.

1

As well as bringing food, water and medicine, they try to help people improve

their _____ .

(d) Eva talks about a part-time job she had.

   (i) Where did Eva work part time when she was at school?

1

   _____

   (ii) Give **two** details about what she did there.

2

   _____

   _____

(e) What started her interest in aid work? State any **one** thing.

1

_____

(f) What did Eva do when she returned to Germany? State any **one** thing.

1

_____

MARKS | DO NOT WRITE IN THIS MARGIN

Item 2

You then hear an interview with Thomas, a German aid worker who works in Malawi in Africa.

(a) For how long has Thomas worked in Africa?   1

_____

(b) Thomas talks about his work.

    (i) Thomas talks about how much he earns. Tick (✓) the correct statement below.   1

	Tick (✓)
Thomas thinks he earns enough.	
Thomas thinks he does not earn enough.	
Thomas would like to earn more.	

    (ii) Why do some of his colleagues in other countries earn more money? State any **one** thing.   1

_____

(c) Thomas talks about life in Malawi. What does he say? State any **three** things.   3

_____

_____

_____

_____

(d) Thomas sometimes feels homesick. Why is this? State any **one** thing.   1

_____

[Turn over

MARKS | DO NOT WRITE IN THIS MARGIN

Item 2 questions (continued)

(e) What is a typical day like for an aid worker in Malawi? Tick (✓) the **two** correct statements.

2

	Tick (✓)
You have to get up before sunrise.	
You have to work long hours.	
He works 15 days a month.	
It is so hot that you can hardly sleep at night.	

(f) Why would Thomas like to work in another country? State **two** things.

2

_____

_____

(g) Why would he like to return to Germany in a few years?

1

_____

[END OF QUESTION PAPER]

MARKS DO NOT WRITE IN THIS MARGIN

ADDITIONAL SPACE FOR ANSWERS

MARKS | DO NOT WRITE IN THIS MARGIN

ADDITIONAL SPACE FOR ANSWERS

National Qualifications 2018

X834/75/13

German
Listening Transcript

MONDAY, 4 JUNE

2:50 PM – 3:20 PM (approx)

This paper must not be seen by any candidate.

The material overleaf is provided for use in an emergency only (eg the recording or equipment proving faulty) or where permission has been given in advance by SQA for the material to be read to candidates with additional support needs. The material must be read exactly as printed.

Instructions to reader(s):

For each item, read the English **once**, then read the German **three times**, with an interval of 1 minute between the three readings. On completion of the third reading, pause for the length of time indicated in brackets after the item, to allow the candidates to write their answers.

Where special arrangements have been agreed in advance to allow the reading of the material, those sections marked **(f)** should be read by a female speaker and those marked **(m)** by a male; those sections marked **(t)** should be read by the teacher.

(t)   Item number one.

You hear a radio report with Eva, an aid worker.

You now have one minute to study the questions for item number one.

(f)   Hallo, ich heiße Eva und ich arbeite als Entwicklungshelferin. Wenn ich von meinem Job erzähle, bewundern mich oft die Menschen. Meine Arbeit ist ja spannend und natürlich auch interessant.

Die Agentur versucht, Menschen auf der ganzen Welt zu helfen. Diese Menschen leben unter schwierigen Umständen und wir bringen ihnen Essen, Wasser und Medikamente. Manchmal versuchen wir auch, die Arbeitschancen der Menschen zu verbessern. Zur Zeit arbeite ich im Westen von Afrika.

Als ich in der Schule war, hatte ich einen Nebenjob in einem Kindergarten in der Stadtmitte. Ich habe am Wochenende von 9 bis Mittag gearbeitet und habe mit den Kindern gesungen und Bücher gelesen. Mein Interesse an der Entwicklungshilfe begann, als ich nach der Schulzeit 6 Monate in Afrika verbracht habe. Dabei habe ich viele neue Leute kennen gelernt, die bei Hilfsorganisationen arbeiteten.

Als ich nach Deutschland zurückkam, habe ich ein Arbeitspraktikum beim Roten Kreuz gemacht. Zu dieser Zeit habe ich zwei Monate in einem Krankenhaus gearbeitet, wo ich sehr viel gelernt habe. Am Schluss habe ich Geografie an der Universität studiert.

(2 minutes)

(t) **Item number two.**

You then hear an interview with Thomas, a German aid worker who works in Malawi in Africa.

You now have one minute to study the questions for item number two.

(f) Seit wann arbeitest du in Afrika Thomas?

(m) Ich arbeite seit Ende meines Studiums hier, also nicht so lange.

(f) Ist der Job gut bezahlt?

(m) Nein, nicht besonders, aber es ist für mich genug. Meine Kollegen, die in anderen Ländern arbeiten, bekommen viel mehr Geld als ich, weil ihre Situationen oft sehr gefährlich sind. Für sie ist das Risiko also viel größer.

(f) Du wohnst im Moment in Malawi. Es ist ein Land, das ich gar nicht kenne. Wie ist das Leben da?

(m) Das Klima ist extremer als in Deutschland. Meistens ist es sehr heiß, aber manchmal gibt es viel Regen. Die Landschaft ist wunderschön — von meinem Fenster aus kann ich die Berge sehen. Das Land ist sehr kulturreich, zum Beispiel gibt es viele traditionelle Tänze und ich liebe die afrikanische Musik hier. Die Leute sind sehr höflich und gastfreundlich.

(f) Von Malawi nach Deutschland sind es über siebentausend Kilometer — das ist eine lange Strecke. Hast du manchmal Heimweh?

(m) Ja, ich muss zugeben, dass ich meine Familie und enge Freunde vermisse. Ich vermisse auch das deutsche Essen und das deutsche Fernsehen.

(f) Die Arbeit ist immer hart, oder?

(m) Ja klar, sehr hart. Vor allem sind die Arbeitsstunden sehr lang — manchmal bis zu 15 Stunden am Tag. Nachts ist es dann so warm, dass man kaum noch schlafen kann.

(f) Möchtest du in der Zukunft in einem anderen Land arbeiten — in Afrika oder in Europa?

(m) Ja, ich kann mir vorstellen, in einem anderen Land zu arbeiten. Es gefällt mir immer, ein neues Land kennen zu lernen und eine neue Sprache zu lernen. In ein paar Jahren habe ich die Absicht, nach Deutschland zurück zu kehren, weil ich sehr gern Kinder dort haben möchte.

(f) Vielen Dank für das Interview, Thomas. Für die Zukunft wünsche ich dir alles Gute.

(2 minutes)

(t) **End of test.**

Now look over your answers.

[END OF TRANSCRIPT]

[BLANK PAGE]

DO NOT WRITE ON THIS PAGE

NATIONAL 5

Answers

NATIONAL 5 GERMAN 2016

Reading

Text 1

(a) <u>Raw</u> material(s)/commodit<u>ies</u>

(b) • Put (a) <u>sticker(s)/sign(s)/message(s)</u>/note(s) saying <u>"No adverts"</u>

   OR

   • Put (a) <u>sticker(s)/sign(s)/message(s)/note(s)</u> on the (house/front) <u>door</u>

   (Candidate needs to mention either the message or where the message is to gain mark)

(c) • They come/are transported by <u>air/plane/are flown</u> in (to Germany) (ignore wrong tenses)

   • This causes (air) pollution

(d) • It (often) <u>looks</u> <u>better/nicer</u> (insist on comparative)

   • It is (usually) (much) cheap<u>er</u>/<u>more</u> reasonably priced/<u>better</u> value/more inexpensive/<u>less</u> expensive/not as expensive as a new one (insist on comparative)

(e) • (They can) exchange/swap <u>clothes</u>

   • <u>Share</u> <u>sports</u> stuff/things/articles/gear/equipment

(f) (i) Try/attempt to <u>repair/fix</u> (broken) things/(a) bike(s)/(a) washing machine(s)

   (ii) Electrical equipment/goods/electronic<u>s</u>/appliance(s)

Text 2

(a) • <u>Hardly</u> any/not many/(a) few/<u>almost</u> no/<u>very</u> little

   • **Tasteless/not tasty/doesn't taste nice/bad tasting (insist on suggestion of negative taste)**

(b) • The pupils/they do the cooking/cook/make their own food/lunch (themselves) (every day)

   • Every two weeks another class is responsible for lunch

   NB: A different class cooks every two weeks — 2 marks

   NB: They cook for two weeks — 1 mark; lacks idea of rotation

(c) • The pupils no longer/don't heat up food/cook in the microwave/eat microwave food/use the microwave (when they go home)

   • They (want to now) cook with/use <u>fresh</u> ingredients/they cook/eat <u>fresh</u> food/cook meals fresh

(d) • Accept/take (on) responsibility/be responsible

   • Work <u>together</u>/<u>with others</u>/collaborate/cooperate/teamwork

   • The cost of food/groceries/meals

(e) • The food is (now) tasty/tastier/delicious/yummy/nice(r)

   • It/the food is now healthy/healthier/good for your health

   • The pupils can get a <u>free</u> second helping/portion/two (meals) for the price of one   **(Any 2 from 3)**

Text 3

(a) • (You can) (always) do <u>what</u> you want/make your own decisions/choose what you want to do

   • (You are) responsible for/in charge of (your own) <u>time</u> management/manage your (own) <u>time</u>

   • (You can) <u>develop/spend time on/try out</u> your own ideas/make your <u>idea(s)</u> a reality   **(Any 2 from 3)**

(b) (i) (At the) <u>Sunday market/market in town</u>

   (NB: market + one piece of information necessary to gain point)

   (ii) • <u>(Quite) a lot of/Many students</u> (have) bought his clothes/wear his clothes

   • He/I began to see/saw his/my clothes/them <u>in/around/about town/in the street</u>

(c) • He had enough money for/bought/got/could afford a <u>used</u>/<u>second hand</u> car

   • (Enough money for an) <u>eight-week</u> trip/journey/holiday through/to Italy

   • He opened/got/had/started a (small) shop (in his home town)   **(Any 2 from 3)**

(d) • (You need) insurance

   • (You need to) repair/fix (a) <u>sewing</u> machine(s)

   (Any 1 from 2)

(e) They wanted to change/alter his jacket(s)/blazer(s) <u>and/or</u> shirt(s)

(f) **BOX 2:** It's worthwhile, although there are also difficulties

   NB: no marks awarded for more than one tick

Writing

General Marking Principles

Candidates will write a piece of extended writing in the modern language by addressing six bullet points. These bullet points will follow on from a job-related scenario. The bullet points will cover the four contexts of society, learning, employability and culture to allow candidates to use and adapt learned material. The first four bullet points will be the same each year and the last two will change to suit the scenario. Candidates need to address these "unpredictable bullet points" in detail to access the full range of marks.

Category	Mark	Content	Accuracy	Language resource — variety, range, structures
Very good	20	The job advert has been addressed in a full and balanced way. The candidate uses detailed language. The candidate addresses the advert completely and competently, **including information in response to both unpredictable bullet points.** A range of verbs/ verb forms, tenses and constructions is used. Overall this comes over as a competent, well-thought-out and serious application for the job.	The candidate handles all aspects of grammar and spelling accurately, although the language may contain one or two minor errors. Where the candidate attempts to use language more appropriate to Higher, a slightly higher number of inaccuracies need not detract from the overall very good impression.	The candidate is comfortable with the first person of the verb and generally uses a different verb in each sentence. Some modal verbs and infinitives may be used. There is good use of adjectives, adverbs and prepositional phrases and, where appropriate, word order. There may be a range of tenses. The candidate uses co-ordinating conjunctions and/or subordinate clauses where appropriate. The language of the e-mail flows well.
Good	16	The job advert has been addressed competently. There is less evidence of detailed language. The candidate uses a reasonable range of verbs/verb forms. Overall, the candidate has produced a genuine, reasonably accurate attempt at applying for the specific job, **even though he/she may not address one of the unpredictable bullet points.**	The candidate handles a range of verbs fairly accurately. There are some errors in spelling, adjective endings and, where relevant, case endings. Use of accents is less secure, where appropriate. Where the candidate is attempting to use more complex vocabulary and structures, these may be less successful, although basic structures are used accurately. There may be one or two examples of inaccurate dictionary use, especially in the unpredictable bullet points.	There may be repetition of verbs. There may be examples of listing, in particular when referring to school/ college experience, without further amplification. There may be one or two examples of a co-ordinating conjunction, but most sentences are simple sentences. The candidate keeps to more basic vocabulary, particularly in response to either or both unpredictable bullet points.

Category	Mark	Content	Accuracy	Language resource — variety, range, structures
Satisfactory	12	The job advert has been addressed fairly competently. The candidate makes limited use of detailed language. The language is fairly repetitive and uses a limited range of verbs and fixed phrases, e.g. *I like, I go, I play*. The candidate copes fairly well with areas of personal details, education, skills, interests and work experience but does not deal fully with the two unpredictable bullet points **and indeed may not address either or both of the unpredictable bullet points.** On balance however the candidate has produced a satisfactory job application in the specific language.	The verbs are generally correct, but may be repetitive. There are quite a few errors in other parts of speech — gender of nouns, cases, singular/plural confusion, for instance. Prepositions may be missing, e.g. *I go the town.* Overall, there is more correct than incorrect.	The candidate copes with the first and third person of a few verbs, where appropriate. A limited range of verbs is used. Sentences are basic and mainly brief. There is minimal use of adjectives, probably mainly after *is* e.g. *Chemistry is interesting.* The candidate has a weak knowledge of plurals. There may be several spelling errors, e.g. reversal of vowel combinations.
Unsatisfactory	8	The job advert has been addressed in an uneven manner and/or with insufficient use of detailed language. The language is repetitive, e.g. *I like, I go, I play* may feature several times. There may be little difference between Satisfactory and Unsatisfactory. **Either or both of the unpredictable bullet points may not have been addressed.** There may be one sentence which is not intelligible to a sympathetic native speaker.	Ability to form tenses is inconsistent. There are errors in many other parts of speech — gender of nouns, cases, singular/plural confusion, for instance. Several errors are serious, perhaps showing mother tongue interference. The detail in the unpredictable bullet points may be very weak. Overall, there is more incorrect than correct.	The candidate copes mainly only with the personal language required in bullet points 1 and 2. The verbs *is* and *study* may also be used correctly. Sentences are basic. An English word may appear in the writing. There may be an example of serious dictionary misuse.

Category	Mark	Content	Accuracy	Language resource — variety, range, structures
Poor	4	The candidate has had considerable difficulty in addressing the job advert. There is little evidence of the use of detailed language. Three or four sentences may not be understood by a sympathetic native speaker. **Either or both of the unpredictable bullet points may not have been addressed.**	Many of the verbs are incorrect. There are many errors in other parts of speech — personal pronouns, gender of nouns, cases, singular/plural confusion, prepositions, for instance. The language is probably inaccurate throughout the writing.	The candidate cannot cope with more than one or two basic verbs. The candidate displays almost no knowledge of the present tense of verbs. Verbs used more than once may be written differently on each occasion. Sentences are very short. The candidate has a very limited vocabulary. Several English words may appear in the writing. There are examples of serious dictionary misuse.
Very poor	0	The candidate is unable to address the job advert. **The two unpredictable bullet points may not have been addressed.** Very little is intelligible to a sympathetic native speaker.	Virtually nothing is correct.	The candidate may only cope with the verbs *to have* and *to be*. Very few words are written correctly in the modern language. English words are used. There may be several examples of mother tongue interference. There may be several examples of serious dictionary misuse.

Listening

Item 1

(a) • A <u>beach</u> house (on Corfu)
   • A <u>holiday</u> flat/apartment (in Spain)
   • A caravan (in the Alps)   **(Any 2 from 3)**

(b) • (You can) live/stay/spend time/be <u>together</u>
   • (You can) <u>share</u> the work/<u>share</u> cooking/<u>share</u> washing up/(You can) <u>all</u> work/<u>all</u> cook/<u>all</u> wash up
   • It's cheaper (than a hotel)
   • (Maybe) your friends might speak another language   **(Any 1 from 4)**

(c) In (the) <u>south</u> (of) France (in a villa)

(d) In a (holiday) brochure/leaflet/pamphlet

(e) • Lying/relaxing/spending time <u>in the sun</u>/<u>sun</u>bathing
   • Swimming <u>in the sea</u>
   • Going to the (large) <u>shopping mall/centre(s)</u> (in the next town)   **(Any 2 from 3)**

(f) **BOX 2:** She's tried it and won't do it again
   NB: no marks awarded for more than one tick

Item 2

(a) His boss/manager

(b) • Holidays <u>abroad</u> are not for her/she does not like holidays <u>abroad</u>
   • You can have a <u>good</u> holiday/time (in Germany)
   • You can go (everywhere) by car/Drive around
   • You can get to know the country/place/countryside/ area/land (better)   **(Any 2 from 4)**

(c) • (To forget) stress/a hectic life/It's stressful/hectic (in the town)
   • Peace/quiet is (very) important to him   **(Any 1 from 2)**

(d) The <u>North Sea</u>/On the <u>north coast</u> (in a holiday home)

(e) The weather is/was bad/It rained (last year)(when he was there)/It rains (all the time)/wet

(f) • It's a compromise
   • It's not (too) far away
   • It's not (too) expensive/it's (very) cheap   **(Any 2 from 3)**

(g) • She was/went/stayed/lived there (already) <u>with her sister</u>/<u>two years ago</u>
   NB: disregard "for two years"; it must be clear that event is in the past
   • She wants (to experience/see) something new   **(Any 1 from 2)**

(h) • (It's good for) shopping/(Good) shopping facilities/ opportunities/The shops
   • At home/At their (own) house/They are not going away

(j) Tidy/clean/clear out/sort out/organise the <u>garage</u>

NATIONAL 5 GERMAN 2017

Reading

Text 1

(a) The best feeling <u>in the world</u>

(b) • She was born with <u>no arms</u>/first person <u>without arms</u> to become a pilot
   • She steers/pilots/controls/flies the plane with her <u>foot/feet</u>
   • She did it against all expectations/(the) odds/she exceeded expectations   **(Any 2 from 3)**

(c) • They were worried/troubled/concerned/had concerns
   • They had reservations/doubts/were hesitant
   • They supported her (to overcome challenges)/they were supportive   **(Any 2 from 3)**

(d) • Climbing <u>with her friend(s)</u>/climbing <u>every week</u>
   • (Goes to/is a member/part of a) <u>sailing/yacht(ing)</u> (club/team) (for many years)
   • Spends <u>every second weekend/every two weekends/</u> by the <u>sea</u>/at the <u>seaside</u>/on the <u>beach</u> (ignore preposition e.g. on/at sea)   **(Any 2 from 3)**

(e) • (Many) <u>interviews/interviewed on TV</u>
   • Spoke at (her old) school(s) about her <u>adventure(s)</u>
   • Organised (free) flights for <u>disabled children</u>   **(Any 2 from 3)**

(f) • Don't/never give up (on your dreams)
   • Live/follow/fulfil your dream/don't dream your life/make your dream a reality   **(Any 1 from 2)**

Text 2

(a) In the <u>neighbouring</u> woods/forest/woods <u>nearby</u>/<u>next</u> to school

(b) • Pupils <u>get to know</u> the (local) area/surroundings/ environment (better)
   • Pupils <u>get to know</u> nature (better)
   • They use their (all) <u>senses</u> (to learn)
   • They learn about (the) <u>natural habitat</u>(s)/<u>biosphere</u> (of insects, plants and animals)/the teacher teaches about <u>insects, plants and animals</u>
   OR
   • They learn about <u>insects, plants and animals</u>
   • It is an <u>important</u> <u>experience</u> (for all children)   **(Any 2 from 5)**

(c) • He hates being indoors/sitting in the class when the sun is shining/when it's sunny/he likes being outside in the sunshine/he enjoys being in the sun/he likes the sun/you get to be in the sun
   • (He gets to) work (together) with his friend(s)
   • They solve/do <u>(a) puzzle(s)/riddle(s)/problem(s)</u> (together)
   • They <u>play</u> (games) (together)
   • <u>Fun</u> to learn about animals   **(Any 2 from 5)**

(d) • The <u>petals</u> of the <u>flowers/blossom</u>

  • The <u>veins</u> of (a) <u>leaf/leaves</u>

  • The <u>bark/crust</u> of (a) <u>tree(s)</u>   **(Any 2 from 3)**

(e) • They <u>spend time</u> in the fresh air/<u>get/gives them</u> fresh air

  • They exercise/move <u>regularly</u>

  • The immune system/<u>becomes stronger/strengthen</u>/ a <u>strong(er)</u> immune system

  • Increase(d) (in) oxygen (levels)

  • They concentrate <u>better/more</u>   **(Any 2 from 5)**

(f) Not (always) reliable/unreliable

Text 3

(a) (Almost) a third

(b) • To do something/it is unusual/different

  • To do something/it is rewarding/worthwhile

  • To gain/get/have/collect (some) work experience

  • To travel/see/explore <u>the world</u>

  • To discover/experience/see/learn about/find (a) new country/countries/land(s) <u>and</u> culture(s)   **(Any 2 from 5)**

(c) (New) challenge(s)/demand(s)

(d) • They are (more) focussed

  • They have (useful) <u>life</u> experience/it is a <u>worthwhile/valuable</u> experience

  • They develop/strengthens (their) (a strong(er)) character/they have a strong(er) character/ personality   **(Any 2 from 3)**

(e) <u>Interesting</u> CV(s)/résumé(s)/application(s)

(f) • (When you showed) initiative/shows

  • (When you) (can) <u>work</u>(ed)/<u>cope(d)</u> under pressure

  • When you <u>worked</u> in a team/team <u>work</u>/team <u>player</u>

  • (When you took on) responsibility/you are responsible (ignore tense)   **(Any 3 from 4)**

Writing

Please see the assessment criteria for Writing on pages 102–104.

Listening

Item 1

(a) On a farm

(b) • It's a vineyard/grow (their own) grapes/vegetables

  • Because his father <u>and</u> grandfather lived/worked here too/it/the farm belongs in his <u>family</u>/ it's a <u>family</u> business/it's been passed down for <u>generations</u>

(c) • They grow (their own) grapes/vegetables (do not accept if answer to part (b))

  • Peaceful/quiet

  • Clean

  • (Very) beautiful/pretty

  • (Great) <u>view</u> of the river/you can <u>see</u> the <u>river</u>

  • His friends live far away/friends don't live nearby

• Because his father and grandfather lived/worked here too/it/the farm belongs in his family/ it's a family business/it's been passed down for generations (do not accept if answer to part (b))   **(Any 2 from 7)**

(d) • It can be lonely (in the evenings)

  • His friends live <u>far away</u>/friends don't live <u>nearby</u> (do not accept if answer to part (c))

  • The <u>public</u> transport is bad/lack of/no <u>public</u> transport/there are few/no travel <u>connections</u>   **(Any 2 from 3)**

(e) He wants to be independent/self-sufficient/to do his own thing/to go on his own/self-reliant/doesn't want to rely on parents

(f) Cinema <u>and</u> youth club/centre/club for young people/ person(s)

Item 2

(a) Three <u>years</u>

(b) • (In a village) on the Austrian <u>border</u>/<u>near</u> Austria

  • With (her) dad (and stepmum)   **(Any 1 from 2)**

(c) • <u>Visited/saw/met/had fun with/went out with</u> friend(s)

  • Did/goes to sport (together)

  • Watched <u>TV</u>

  • Chatted

  • Went to (a) BBQ(s)

  • Laughed (lots)

  • Went camping

  • Went to shops/ice-cream parlour/cafe   **(Any 2 from 8)**

(d) • Her friend(s)

  • The <u>fresh</u> air

  • The security/it is safe(r)

  • Slower pace of life/it is not so hectic (in the country)/more hectic/stressful <u>in the town</u>   **(Any 2 from 4)**

(e) • There is/are <u>no</u> bus(es)/can't take/get a bus

  • There is not much happening <u>for young people</u>/ there's not a lot/nothing <u>for young people</u> (to do)   **(Any 1 from 2)**

(f) • It has everything you need

  • It is <u>never/not</u> boring

  • (You can go to the) cinema

  • There are (big) shopping <u>centre</u>(s)/<u>good</u> (for) shopping/<u>good</u> shops   **(Any 2 from 4)**

(g) She got a job there (quickly)/more job opportunities (than in the county)/could find a job/found work (quickly)/<u>more</u> jobs/it was hard(er) to get a job in the country

(h) • In the city/(big)town

  • Free time <u>opportunities</u> (there)/(things) to do

NATIONAL 5 GERMAN 2018

Reading

Text 1

1. (a) • There's (too/so much) noise <u>and</u> traffic/(it's too) noisy/loud <u>and</u> there is (too much) traffic

    OR

    • There is not much traffic <u>and</u> noise where he lives now

   (b) • It's <u>physically</u> tiring/demanding/straining/strenuous/challenging/hard <u>for your body</u>

    • It's often (incredibly/unbelievably) dirty/filthy

   (c) (i) • The <u>theory and practice of agriculture/farming/working the land</u>

    • Learn about the <u>different/various/all aspects/sides</u> of life on a <u>farm</u>

      NB: For 2 marks to be awarded, reference must be made to farming/agriculture <u>at least once</u>

    (ii) • He hopes to have/own his own farm (in the future)

    • It's <u>valuable</u> experience   **(Any 1 from 2)**

   (d) • <u>Meat and milk/dairy products</u> are not profitable (any more)/don't bring in (big) profits/don't make money/(only) bring in small profits/bring/make no profit

    • There's <u>less/little/hardly any/fewer/not much financial help/aid</u> (from the government)

    OR

    • <u>Less/little/hardly any/fewer/not much</u> (financial) <u>help</u> from the <u>government</u>

   (e) • They are expensive/it costs a lot/you have to spend a lot (of money) (on them)

    • They need to be repaired <u>constant(ly)/permanently/a lot/continually/always/often</u>

    OR

    • <u>High</u> maintenance

      NB: *"Expensive to repair"* should be awarded 1 mark

Text 2

2. (a) • <u>Develop</u> (their) creativity

   (b) • It is (an important part of) <u>youth/young/teen</u> culture

   (c) • In underground stations

   (d) (i) • (Some people find graffiti) (real/genuine) works of art/art work/art

    • (Graffiti makes boring, grey walls/buildings)/(it is) lively/livelier/alive/colourful/more colourful/bright/brighter

    (ii) • They find graffiti/it is <u>aggressive</u>

    • Graffiti/it <u>spoils/ruins/wastes the buildings</u> (in town)   **(Any 1 from 2)**

   (e) • <u>Removal/Cleaning</u> of graffiti costs a lot/(€35—50 million) <u>every/each/a/per year</u>

      NB: There has to be an implication of a lot of money

   (f) • <u>Repair/restore/refurbish</u> the wall <u>paintings/art</u>

   (g) • It is an (international) symbol/sign of freedom/liberty

      [must be idea that the East-Side-Gallery <u>is</u> the symbol]

    • Tourists can see <u>more than/over a hundred/hundreds of pictures/drawings</u>

    • Tourists can see art/pictures/drawings/artists from <u>all over the world</u>

      NB: *Tourists can see hundreds of pictures from all over the world* should be awarded 2 marks
                        (Any 2 from 3)

Text 3

   (a) (i) • The (new)(school) rector/the head teacher/principal

    (ii) • (While visiting a) (twin/partner) <u>school in Brazil</u>

   (b) • <u>Happy/glad</u> (to have their parents/them in school/there)

    • They wanted to show what they had done/learned (in lessons/school)

   (c) • <u>Not all/many (children)</u> are/were keen/enthusiastic (to have their parents in school)

    • Parents need a <u>police</u> <u>certificate/permit</u> (if they spend time in a school)/need a <u>background</u> check (from the police)/a check from the <u>police</u>

    • It can't be organised in a day/It takes a long time to organise   **(Any 2 from 3)**

   (d) • A few <u>parents</u> (who work for firms in the town) spoke with the children/pupils (about the world of work)/the children were spoken to about <u>the world of work</u>/children got to speak/learn/hear about <u>the world of work</u>

    • They have a network of (good) contacts/contacts (with firms and employers) (in the town)

   (e) • Young people are learning <u>more</u> about <u>the/their world</u> (what we did in the past)

    • Children have <u>fun/enjoy</u> <u>working together/collaborating/cooperating</u> with their (class)mates

    • The <u>relationship/connection</u> between the teacher <u>and</u> the class/pupils OR the <u>atmosphere</u> (in class) is relaxed/easy going   **(Any 2 from 3)**

Writing

Please see the assessment criteria for Writing on pages 102—104.

Listening

Item 1

1. (a) • People admire her (for doing it)

    • (It's) exciting

    • (It's) interesting   **(Any 1 from 3)**

(b) • All over the world

(c) • <u>Chances</u> of employment/work/(finding) a job/
job/work/employment <u>prospects/opportunities/
employability/finding</u> work/ways to find a job/
(education so that) they can get jobs/work

(d) (i) • (She worked) in a <u>nursery/kindergarten/
playgroup</u> (in the town centre)

 (ii) • She <u>sang</u> (with the children)

   • She <u>read</u> (books) (with the children)

(e) • She went to <u>Africa</u> <u>for 6 months</u>/spent <u>6 months</u> in
<u>Africa</u>/went to <u>Africa</u> <u>after (finishing) school</u>

 • She <u>got to know</u> many people in Africa (who worked
with aid agencies)   **(Any 1 from 2)**

(f) • Did work experience/placement/worked/
volunteered at <u>the Red Cross</u>

 • <u>Worked</u>/did <u>work experience</u> in a <u>hospital</u>
(for 2 months)

 • (Studied/did) <u>geography at university</u>   **(Any 1 from 3)**

Item 2

(a) • Since the end of her studies/end of school/
university

 • Not (so/too/for) long   **(Any 1 from 2)**

(b) (i) • Thomas thinks he earns enough.

 (ii) • (Because) they work in <u>dangerous</u> situations/it's
<u>dangerous</u>

   • (Because) the <u>risk</u>(s) is/are big(ger)/great(er)/
it's <u>risky/riskier</u>   **(Any 1 from 2)**

(c) • The climate/weather is (more) extreme (than in
Germany)

 • (Most of the time) it's <u>very/really</u> hot/warm

 • (Sometimes) it rains <u>a lot</u>/there is <u>heavy</u> rain

 • The landscape/scenery/countryside is <u>beautiful/
wonderful/pretty</u>

 • He/You can <u>see</u> the <u>mountains</u> (from his window)

 • The country/It is <u>rich in culture/a lot of culture/
full of culture/very cultural</u>/The people are <u>very</u>
cultural/cultured

 • There are lots of <u>traditional</u> dances

 • He <u>likes/enjoys</u> the <u>African</u> music/he <u>likes/enjoys</u>
the music <u>there/in Malawi</u>

 • The <u>people/they</u> are polite

 • The <u>people/they</u> are welcoming/hospitable/guest
friendly   **(Any 3 from 10)**

(d) • Misses his family

 • Misses his (close) friends

 • Misses the <u>German</u> food/food <u>at home</u>

 • Misses the <u>German</u> television/television <u>at home</u>
                                                 (Any 1 from 4)

(e) • BOX 2 (You have to work long hours)

 • BOX 4 (It's so hot that you can hardly sleep at night)

(f) • (He likes) to <u>get to know/experience</u> a new/the
country/land/it

 • (He likes) to learn a new/different/another language.

(g) • To have a child/children/kids/(start a) family

Acknowledgements

Permission has been sought from all relevant copyright holders and Hodder Gibson is grateful for the use of the following:

Image © patpat/Shutterstock.com (2016 Reading page 2);
Image © Guy Shapira/Shutterstock.com (2016 Reading page 4);
Image © wavebreakmedia/Shutterstock.com (2016 Reading page 6);
Image © michaeljung/Shutterstock.com (2017 Reading page 2);
Image © Hurst Photo/Shutterstock.com (2017 Reading page 4);
Image © Halfpoint/Shutterstock.com (2017 Reading page 6);
Image © olly/stock.adobe.com (2018 Reading page 2);
Image © Birkit Kinder/DACS 2018 via Abel Tumik/Shutterstock.com (2018 Reading page 4);
Image © kmiragaya/stock.adobe.com (2018 Reading page 6).